BREAKING DOWN THE SURFACE OF THE WORLD

Part I:
Geography

Jack Grapes

BOMBSHELTER PRESS
Los Angeles, 1996

ISBN 0-941017-48-6

This is a work in progress. *Breaking Down the Surface of the World* is a long poem sequence in 3 parts: "Geography," "History," and "Physics." Some of the sections in Part I have previously appeared in slightly different form in *Poetry/LA*, *Beyond Baroque Magazine*, *Pinchpenny*, *Tsunami*, and *The New Orleans Review*.

Cover design by Judith James

My thanks to Michael Andrews for his usual advice and help in designing the book, and to the poets in our Thursday night group for their suggestions and support, and as always, to my wife Lori, for her critical eye and compassionate heart.

This book was printed at
Gemini Graphics in Marina del Rey, California

Bombshelter Press
P.O. Box 481266
Bicentennial Station
Los Angeles, CA 90048

for Josh

my father's grandson

ॐ

Breaking Down the Surface of the World

Geography

Sometimes I am very small.
In another life.
Low to the ground.
Eyes with clubs.
Axe-handles.
Drums.

I see what's up.
I run from one end of the room
to the other.

There.
Safe.
Thunder.
The long shadow of wood.
Belts accreted 'round cratons
and flung across the island arcs
consuming plate boundaries.

There's a red bed in the corner.

Outside I can see the zinc tubs
my mother does the washing in.
Through crust and bone,
from trench to arc,
she hangs her flesh out to dry
and is nowhere to be found.

Each knife has a name.
Butcher.
Bread.
Paring.
Every door a lock;
key and bolt,
latch and chain.

Outside the window
lines of cars
their yellow headlights
in the bright sun.
My father drives among them.
He waves to me.
I wave back.

Every morning

the same size.
The house so quiet:
Brain torture.
Shuffled about.
Eyeballs into cement.
Neptune bursting into flame.
Jupiter, a perfection of toes.

Old rocks within younger rocks
line the front yard where I bury
little things
I find around the house.
Less familiar the longer I hold them.

Big wood.
Axe-handles.
Drums.

b

The mailman pushes his cart
packed with letters and magazines
and parks it next door.

I'm out here breathing
waving goodbye, saying hello,
getting the mail
not even waiting for the mailman.
To meet no train that stops.
Hands in my pockets
rocking back and forth on my heels
as a car goes by full of fish,
swarms of kids on their way to swimming lessons—
the last swimming lesson of the summer.

There goes Mars
barfing up suicide.
There goes Pluto
gristle in the brain.

In another life
toothpicks investigate the courage of seashells.
Rearranged like furniture.
Nighttime, bedtime, bloodtime, moontime.
Burglar bars, daddy bars, baby bars, bloody bars.
The slavery of the head.

A thin blanket, green with stripes
lies among the granite-like rocks
in the backyard.
Layers of crust in the toaster.
On the mantle above the fireplace with no fire,
golf trophies,
souvenir shields,
belt-buckles,
white-china plate with ripple marks
steadily losing heat
to gold cuff-links in its center
flashing reflections of sunlight
as I walk by.
Venus as I walk by.
Mercury as I walk by.
Uranus as I walk by.
I walk by looking for permanence.

The chairs get up during the night
and dance.
They vanish beneath the ocean water
and bathroom basins.
I feel the shift in the house.
Low rolling surfaces.
Blocks of various shapes and sizes,
raised, lowered, tilted.
Some notion as to their character
still deeper and worn down.

When I try to reach into their sleep
it is like freezing my teeth
on refrigerator water
left in a frosted milk bottle.
The sun is so red today.
Ernie says don't look directly into it.

We find a piece of cardboard,
prick a hole with a pencil
and peep through it.
See the red sun and go blind.
Everyone goes blind.
We bump into each other in the streets,

bump into the trees,
bump into houses.

"I'm blind," yells A.J.
He's excited.
He walks stiff-legged, hands stretched out,
groping the air in front of him.
"Me, too," yells my brother.
Everyone's lined up to go blind,
wanting to look into the sun.
Darryl falls into the gutter and laughs.
"I can't see either," he says.
We're delirious with blindness.

We sit on the curb
and watch the cars go by;
same cars, same drivers.
We wave at them, they wave back.
I look at a broken coke bottle.
A.J. stares at old lady Senac
rocking in her rocker
on the front porch across the street.
No one's in the mood to tease her.
Darryl watches the tree out front,

my brother looks at me.
We can all see again.

Later, I dig a small trench in the yard,
fill it with water,
watch the displacement of rock and dirt,
their strike–slip movements
as they slide down into the murk.

One night there is a sudden distress.
I'm being picked up in the thin green blanket
and thrown across the room
to land in a cardboard suitcase.
The big steel ship stale with fatigue.
The suitcase filled with dirt
and fingernails,
dry crackly pieces of skin.
My own skin.
Bits of blood where the break was too deep,
dried rust against the light–veined brown.
Someone pours in water.
The chips of skin loosen and turn soft,
hold flat against my forehead and cheeks.
A new face shuffled around the original crust,

shifted beyond recognition.
Was it a sort of slag on the surface
of the case when its rocky crust
first took form?
Or did it change along a zone of weakness
too subtle and precise to contain
even the smallest scream?

My father snaps the case shut.
My mother retreats into the closet;
whimpers, laughs, pecks at the door.
She's mad.
I see this clearly.
Her madness flourishes like an umbrella.
Already it's too late.
While you gallop through your sleep
each night
trying to understand love
and prevent the last sour dream
from spilling onto your pillow,
my mother and I slash at your shadow:
she, pecking at the door;
me, pounding on the inside of the suitcase.
One of us can not get out

without the other.

All in another life.
Neptune. Mars.
Fat women raise their dresses
to dance over skinnier naked bodies.

>   *no platform. no*
>   *ridges.*
>   *her breast is a rift.*

She steps lightly over each one;
penises rising as she bends
and strokes them, down,
far below the limits of observation.

One woman is up, the other down;
legs kick high as the fat jiggles
and rolls out the shadows
that catch in their folds.

Red splotches appear on their thighs,
on their breasts, flushed and bruised,
never hotter than they are now.

A thrust oceanward.
Iron formations give way to red beds.
Inside, where my defective heart
pumps rift systems in alkaline complexes
that drive deeper into the interior,
I feel the heat acting as a thermal buffer
to everything closing down around me.
I hide in the basement,
attain a degree of rigidity.

How far am I from the spreading center
of the room as flesh and cotton float
among the pillows and blankets?
At the edge of the room
with my back to the door
I shine with the head of a new deformation.
The flare of a match.
Magnetic polarities shift,
each band moving outward in turn
sizzling from my body.
Fractures everywhere.
I move from one end of the room to the other.

Never again in the spreading center.

Never again the single place to turn in.
It's one end or the other.
Folds upon folds upon folds.
My transformation into granite.

C

Winter is a bright moon
hanging, as the horses kick dogs
that worry them in their sleep.
Everyone is cold.
Strangers wave icicles
by the fire;
Mutants everywhere
mate with others not their kind.
It is a terrible night.
No one can read yet.

Uncle Charles takes me in his new convertible.
We ride around and look up at the stars.
"That's the North Star," he says.
I ask him where the South Star is.
"There is no South Star."
When he dies, they tell me he's gone.
To the North Star, I think.

There's always something someone's not telling me.

Cold dust and stone.
My father comes home drunk
and smashes the mirror in the bathroom.
Chunks of glass in the sink.
When I look, there's my face,
looking in so many different directions.
Water I cannot put my hands into.
Sea shells in the Rocky Mountains.
Marine deposits on the plains of Kansas.
The remains of fig trees in Greenland.
Glacial debris in Australia and Brazil.

One night my mother bundles me up in a blanket
and calls a cab to take us to *maMa's* house.
She lives far away in Metairie,
where the train comes from.
I tell the cab driver:
"My father's coming to chop our heads off."
Even with the windows shut, I can feel the cold.
There's the sign for Ritz crackers.
The first word I learn to read.
Everything is ritzy.

I begin to put one and one together.

The concept of a random universe.
The idea of causality.
Is it one or the other or both?
Red and Yellow make Orange.
Blue and Yellow make Green.
Green and Orange make Brown.
That's something you can count on.
When I color, I press hard on the edges,
soft on the inside.
I can breathe inside the colors.
I spell my name.

d

The child studies the mirror, then the face.
Which is no longer the face of the child,
but man,
waiting in the winter of the mirror
to be born.

Snow melts as soon as I touch it.
Most of it melting in the air
melting when it touches something warmer
like the sidewalk
or my fingers
and I hold my hand
inside the freezer as long as I can
and go out running
to keep the frozen flakes
clustered in my palm
to catch sight of the pattern
science books showed.
By comparison
my flesh sizzles

beneath the crystal
of ice.

For a long time it is winter.
In the mirror, way back in the background,
my mother walks back and forth,
putting on her girdle, taking off her girdle.
My brother cuts his finger on some broken glass.
My father drinks from the bottle.
My sister isn't born yet.

e

I touch everything
like flies, like rivers,
like the black pearl
stored away in boxes
ornamented with gold rope.
What will I let myself remember today?
The box with the pair of scissors
varnished black?
Or the one with dried grains of corn?
I open the door.
Eat with great deliberation.
The house burns day and night.
A cow is no longer a cow.
A sack of grain no longer a month's food.
The black pearl reminds me
of something else.
In the mirror, I watch myself.
The beauty that is born
stands on two feet
even in the slime of creation

Breaking Down

and sings as it moves
among beasts.

f

We are crossing the Suru River
looking for Yaks, the primitive cow.
The pilot's head is on my lap
and I'm flying the plane.
With enough fuel
I can take the Himalayas:
the white goats climbing the crag.
The animals below us
immune to the land,
look up at our noise
but barely.
Then back to climbing,
to grazing.
The world beneath their feet
their one earthly thing.

g

Someone has gone
and overturned the lake again.
I don't understand this one word here,
he says.
Neither do I, which is why I keep it in.
But countless things escape
so easily out of you, he gasps.
Are you gasping?
Actually gasping?

And someone's given birth
to a brilliant lizard.

Here is some news:
Today is meat.
The cows, letters etched
into their hides, play
the alphabet game:
Guess who I am?
It starts with a C.
Once the fastest animal
in the world.

Breaking Down

i

What nigger meant
and kike
and dago
and polack
and wop
and jew-boy
and sheeny
and litvak
and mick
and crab.
Old man Seenac in his ragged undershirt
shows hairy underarms
as he stands by the kitchen door
yelling out at me you little kike
bastard jew-boy.
I loved his daughter Linda,
under the house
spreading her legs
to catch a peek of red, hairless vagina
and pissing in the dry dirt, both of us

pledging someday to marry:
the kike and the dago.
And the blacks all around us,
mother goose nuns at the corner.
Division   division   division.
Clean spit against the windshield
of a 1947 Dodge.
Bicycle down to Prytania Street
and watch the girls roller skate.
Catch a snowball on the way back.
Dago street where Rosalie lived
sucking the boys off down in the basement,
boys who didn't even know yet
what it was to come.
Did you get the feeling, A.J. asked,
and we all lied, even then.

j

A dream: I am carrying the large lizard
over the back of my neck like a stole
up the stairs and into a room
filled with my friends.
They're on fire but they're laughing,
eating with both hands.
A vat of tomato sauce boils on the stove.
I dump the lizard into it.
Half of him hangs out
struggling to escape.
He makes no sound,
but his jaws snap and his body
swings across the rim
like a loose hose gushing water.
I take him out
and eat:
It's good.
It tastes just like lizard.

In the evenings I come home
and there's my mother
laying the ties out
in regular rows on the kitchen table.
Blue ties.
Nothing but blue silk ties.

My father boards the airplane,
and flies
over the mountains.
For there is no eminence on earth
not subject to erosion,
the inexorable
destroyer.
"When is he coming home,"
my sister asks.
We go outside
and watch the sky.
My father waves.
I wave back.

1

My brothers and I scoot into the corner
around the kitchen table
and eat our steaming chicken noodle soup.
No one talks, no one breathes,
just my brothers slurping
soup
and me, sitting in the steam
saying the words to myself:
nigger
wop
jew-boy
dago
polack
kike
sheeny
litvak
mick.
The words roll off the tongue
with a strange kind of music.

At night, we take our shovels
and sneak into the backyard
and start digging.
In the glare of the moon
I can see A.J.'s face sweating.
Darryl wants the words as bad as I do.
He's got the big shovel.
Everyone wants the big shovel,
but Darryl's the biggest
with actual muscles in his arms
so no one takes it from him yet.
Shit comes first.
We stand in a circle around the hole
looking at it.
I hear Mr. Higbee open the ice-box
in his kitchen next door.
We stand very quiet,
our cheeks streaked with mud.
The light in Mr. Higbee's kitchen goes out
and we resume looking down at Shit.
The word glows in the darkness.
A.J. reaches into the hole
and picks it up.
He brings Shit up and shows it to us.

I like the way it looks with the capital S.
Darryl says keep digging.
The moon passes behind a dark cloud
and we dig.
Out comes fuck with a pop.
No capital.
The word amazes us, we are stunned by its beauty.
The k remains partly buried
but everyone knows it's a k,
everyone knows it's fuck.
The breathless wonder of seeing it like that.
I'd say, "fuck, that's beautiful," but the word
isn't in my hand yet.
I dare to pick it up first.
I shake the dirt off the k
and hold it up in my hand.
fuck, says A.J.
fuck, says Darryl.
fuck, says Karl.
fuck, I say.
The sound of it stuns us.
The mystery of the word deepens
the more I say it.
The more we all say it.

fuck. fuck. fuck.
Louder and louder.
The lights in the houses go on.
We dig faster, and deeper.
My shovel hits cunt.
A.J. unearths dick and screw and piss.
We're pulling the words up and saying them aloud
and all across the neighborhood
the lights in the houses go on
and we're saying the words even louder.
fuck. And
cunt.
Say them with the capital letter, I yell.
The power of it all surges
like an electrical storm,
the houses tremble in the dark and fall down.
If they were cities, they'd fall, too.

We dig deeper.
All the bones of the words come out of the earth.
The moon is full and bright again.
We can see as if we'd been blind.
The words lie in the palms of our hands,
murderous, horrible, beautiful words.

Maps bring the greatest pleasure:
a faded navigational chart;
an authentic medieval portolano;
outlines of the Mediterranean;
maps of the flat earth;
the ocean: the universal cataract.
Under the last, translated from the Spanish:

> *"The nature of waters*
> *is always to communicate*
> *and to reach a common level.*
> *This is their mystery."*

ת

We are crushed beneath his weight.
The men go to Grande Isle
and bring home giant fish packed in ice.
But I do not eat the fish.
I want to know the secret.
What makes his breath change,
What makes him leave in the night,
What makes him
the captain of the boat.
He tells me stories of his days
on the streets of New York
and his days as a cowboy
wounded out West,
and nursed back to health by Juanita,
the Mexican woman who loved him.
He tells us tales of throwing bricks
from the roofs of tenements,
with Beany, and Shorty, and Lefty, and Moe;
onto the heads of the policemen below,
of running with a gang called Murderer's Row.

Which do I believe?

From the backseat of a '49 maroon Mercury,
I watch him drive the car
and never once does he hit a tree,
never once do we go sailing off a cliff,
or run out of gas in the middle of the forest.
He drives us in our little egg,
the force of love blinding us to his pain.

When he walks, the rooms shake.
In the kitchen after work
he writes long columns of numbers
on a yellow piece of paper,
the code fathers know,
the secret formula
in a world for which there is no map,
no permanent state of nature,
no gene that carries
a knack for direction.

He wraps packets of money
inside the yellow paper
and wraps that with a rubber band.

In winter he stands on the prow of the ship
and faces into the wind,
the smooth skin taut against the bone.
Yet nothing is permanent.
New plateaus warp toward the sky.
New torrents obliterate the land.
He sails off in his boat
and leaves us in the kitchen
to add numbers by ourselves.

The men who are his friends
carry him home
and put him on the sofa.
He smells of whiskey,
lies there with his eyes closed,
but still he drives the car,
and still we fly through space in our little egg.

I tell him I never saw a purple cow
but that I hope one day to be one.
Is he dead or sleeping?
He puts his hand out and touches my head.
Does he know it's me,
or is he feeling for the wheel?

Which do I believe?

My mother sings:

> *Dormez-vous, dormez-vous,*
> *ding dong ding.*

This part of me is a continent—
the mysterious earth,
the lava that holds mountains together,
the richest traveler sold to silk,
the flutes,
the bellies of women,
the pubic hairs,
the secrets too old to forget,
the child
who stands at the end
of the hallway
afraid his father might die.

I leave my father in his hospital bed
and wait for the elevator alone.
The neat walls pucker up like fish.
For the first time
it is possible to sit and count:
moons, stars, inevitable shadows;
Neptune, Jupiter, Uranus, Pluto.
Starfish, seahorse, catfish, seagull;
the frescos, the billboards,
the skywriters sputtering up there
selling suntan oil.
There goes Mars. There goes Venus.
All fall down.

q

In the morning we are children again.
Someone knocks and says
"You have to get up
and get dressed
and advance in the ashen world."

Mother wipes the frost from the windows.
I scoot out from under the icy sheets.
Poles migrate rapidly
over different parts of the room.
Imprisoned in the paved cities.
Graves in caverns of age-old rock.
To penetrate the disguises of the visible world.
Born on this strange craft,
the awful vibrations of its deck,
clinging to the surface of this sphere.

The enormous room.
Two pennies lie on the floor near the bed.
One, a black war penny.

We take war stamps from the book
to pay for gasoline.
I hide in the backseat.

There's a giant birthday cake.
Sunday, October 23, 4004 B.C.
"Fossil discoveries are
devices planted by the devil
to delude us," he says.
But we go to work in the ever-lasting Fire.
A.J. carries his briefcase full of rocks.
Darryl pokes around in his lunch bag
full of some iron-magnesium silicate like olivine,
a heavy, greenish crystalline substance.
"I can't eat this!" he yells.
I pour out my vial upon the sun
and men are scorched by the great heat
and cities of the plain fall at our feet.
All the towering peaks we know lie crumpled
on the ocean floor.
There goes Betelgeuse. There goes Antares.

We walk to school looking for bugs
to put in our lunch bags.

We begin to advance in the ashen world.

r

The class room is filled with maps.
I can't remember where they said the bathroom was.
Afraid to ask again,
I walk into every room
and back out, looking for the door.
The seniors bulge and hold the walls up,
the hydraulic monarchies advance
beyond the steep hills,
the steepness of the land
shown by layer tints,
contour lines, relief shadings,
while the true character of the land
is difficult to infer.
Back into the small desk,
I stare bluntly at the folds and faults
of the techtonic map
thumbtacked below the blackboard.

The teacher reads out of a book:
> *"Early Pleistocene deformations*
> *brought about a widespread emergence."*

I can see her stockings,
her chubby thighs, the five rivers,
the walls of fortified cities!

She cups both hands before her.

Gunpowder!   The bayonet!   The stirrup!

The atom bomb!   The coming of the clock!

Printing!

I squeeze against the metal frame of the desk.
I grip the edges of the desk top,
rippling against geometry
that shows each rise and fall of rock,
and release, and release the warm urine
along the line of my leg,
down to the socks,
slow to burn its way to my toes.
The piss, the hot piss, the fundamental nature
of the continent, piss after piss after piss,
Russian piss and Chinese piss and Roman piss
along the skin itching as the bell rings

and everyone grabs their schoolbags but me,
squatting in the warm pool that continues to build
in the piss of the piss by the piss
warmest of arms all around my body
bellowing up from the earth.

S

Since winter,
the windows have been closed.
I open the box of coins:
human profiles
blurred by the touch of hands.

If a woman were here,
I would obey her.

Geography is so bare.
Like a wet fish,
the thumbprint on the refrigerator
wiggles across the chrome.
It's midnight.
They march up to the door
and Yippee! the soldiers are home.
Who minds their muddy boots.

Ah, but a hundred miles away
the city is being eaten.
Who's in charge
of burning all these papers?
The sheets and suits
with no names attached,
false teeth in a cup
and Wednesday, missing with the rest.
No one puts anything away.
Sheets of dead skin crunch underfoot.
Static on the radio,

fire drills,
children in the street
hitting other children
with long cracking sticks.

Who is going to marry
at a time like this.

u

Jaunty is the word
for someone who dies before you were born.
That's my second cousin Alfred
and Alfred's father, and their first car.
Everyone over there is crossing the street.
There's the blue tablecloth
we'll fold on the old folds, if possible.

And Uncle Joe or Poppa or Mr. Lettelier:
look how young I look
bordered in white,
yellowing.
Scotch tape on four corners
facing Cockeyed-Jenny
on the other page,
just off the boat from Antwerp,
afraid to let go of the rail
as she walks down
the gangplank
to touch the ground of New York,
the New World.

V

The erotic force
        shapes the better performance;
another range of available styles.

I am pigeon-toed to the sun
        and look up at it,
neck stretched, holding up by torch
                the power
between thighs   entire plates
        concealed beneath the ridges
                of my skull.

My arms point out some
        flying object
over there   by the blue cloud
        just   about
to eat the reindeer's head.

Looking out from the sloping roof
        through branches of the neighbor's
                sycamore

over housetops
and the streetlights
between houses,
I move to the edge

ready to take off.

W

I don't pray for miracles.
I put pebbles in a box
and bury them near the magnolia tree
because it is messy and too sweet,
as imperfect as the rest of us.
The comfort in that.
And in the ritual of school,
of pencils and paper and swivel chairs and chalk.
Lines painted on asphalt I follow
to the bathroom, to the library, to lunch.
When my father dies
I don't look inside the coffin.
I hear the sound of dirt hitting the coffin
with my eyes closed.
Then I am driven, in a line
of dark cars, into my life as a man.

Geese fly south.
Swans skirt the perfect edge
of ponds,
their long necks
an arc of feathers.
Their wake opens outward
in the water.
I am outward in my gaze:
the perfect incision
between lava and rock.

In the palm of my hand
I mix a little paste;
a little blood
a little zinc.
Some of us have weak eyes.
The blind bump into everything.
Mix in a little sand,
a little grass.
Some gunpowder.

Anything living will do.
Parts of the body
fly across the sky.
There goes femur.
There goes backbone.
There is little need to remember numbers.
Only the naming becomes important.
St. Peter's Sandstone.
London Clay.
Montmarte Gypsum.

You can read the paper
and catch up on everything,
though in some countries
they only print the truth.
When I make soup
I sing to myself in the kitchen:

    dormez-vous, ding dong ding.

The song is what gives me away.

Now on the table
all my friends in ties
waving goodbye.
And so much time taken
to learn again
what we knew
from each other
and forgot.
It's still daylight
but I can see the moon.
Almost,
or so it seems,
transparent.
Not even a full moon.
But a full moon.

Z

Vows:

We're going to get married
and have kids
and live together
and be bloody.

Books by Jack Grapes:

A Savage Peace
Two Poets (with Shael Herman)
Seven Is a Frozen Number
Perchance, in all your travels, have you ever been
        to Pittsburgh?
Termination Journal
Breaking On Camera
AfterImage (with Kita Shantiris)
Some Life
Presto! (with Vern Maxam)
Trees, Coffee, and the Eyes of Deer
and the running form, naked, Blake
Breaking Down the Surface of the World

Jack Grapes is a poet, playwright, actor, teacher, and the editor of ONTHEBUS, a literary journal. He's received several NEA Fellowships in Literature and numerous Artist-in-Residence grants from the California Arts Council. He wrote and starred in *Circle of Will*, a comedy about the lost years of Will Shakespeare which ran for several years in Los Angeles and won two theatre critics awards, including Best Comedy. *The Los Angeles Times* called it a play that went "way beyond mere entertainment; Grapes has created an intelligent piece of theatre which peers into the very foundations of drama itself. It is one of the cleverest original works seen in a long time."

Of *Trees, Coffee, and the Eyes of Deer*, Dennis Cooper wrote: "His work is generous, passionate, as full-bodied as a meal and yet delicate as a fog, something which never falls between him and his writing, between his work and us. This unique usage of poetry, this humane artistic ideal, conscious or unconscious, of what poetry should be, is his own. Ours too, if we are wise enough to receive it."

He was born and raised in New Orleans, received a BA in English and History, and an MFA in Theatre from Tulane University. He now lives in Los Angeles with his wife, Lori, and his son, Joshua.